CONTENTS

A COUNTRY AT WAR

From September 1939 to August 1945 Britain fought in World War II. The fighting took place all over the world, on land, at sea and in the air.

► Map of Europe in 1942, showing the countries occupied by Germany and its allies. For a long time Britain stood alone.

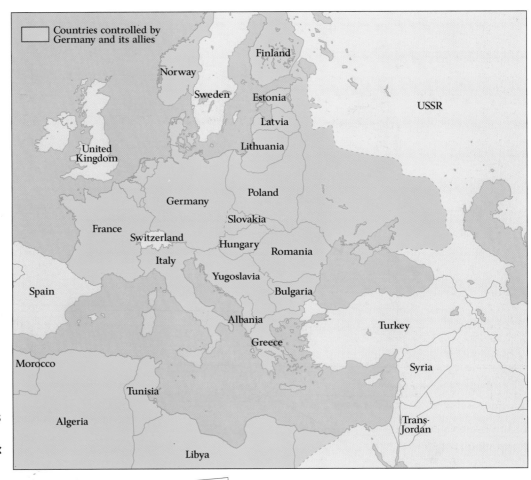

Countries controlled by Germany and its allies

Finland
Norway
Sweden
Estonia
Latvia
Lithuania
USSR
United Kingdom
Poland
Germany
Slovakia
France
Switzerland
Hungary
Romania
Italy
Yugoslavia
Spain
Bulgaria
Albania
Turkey
Greece
Morocco
Syria
Tunisia
Algeria
Trans-Jordan
Libya

▼ While many men were away fighting, women did their jobs. This woman took over her husband's milk round.

After almost six years, the 'Allies' (Britain and France with their empires, Russia and the USA) defeated the 'Axis' countries (Germany, Italy and Japan). Although there was no fighting in mainland Britain, the war affected everyone's lives. Millions joined the armed forces. Others did voluntary work. Everyone, from children to grannies, had to work hard and do their bit for the war effort.

ON THE
TRAIL

WORLD WAR II
IN BRITAIN

STEWART ROSS

W
FRANKLIN WATTS
LONDON • SYDNEY

© 1999 Franklin Watts
First published in Great Britain by
Franklin Watts
96 Leonard Street
London EC2A 4XD

Franklin Watts Australia
45-51 Huntley Street
Alexandria
NSW 2015
Australia

ISBN 0 7496 3231 3 (hbk)
ISBN 0 7496 3589 4 (pbk)

Dewey Decimal Classification: 941·084
A CIP record for this book is available
from the British Library

Printed at Oriental Press, Dubai, U.A.E.

Planning and production by Discovery Books Ltd
Editors: Helena Attlee and Helen Lanz
Design: Simon Borrough
Consultant: Tim Copeland
Art: Stuart Carter, Stefan Chabluk

Photographs: English Heritage Photographic
Library: 10; Hulton Getty: 13; The Imperial War
Museum: 4, 6 (bottom), 7 (both), 8, 11 (bottom),
14, 16 (top), 18, 19 (both), 20, 21 (bottom), 23 (bottom), 24 (bottom), 25 (right); Alex Ramsay:
cover 2, 5 (bottom), 11 (top), 12, 17 (top), 21 (top),
23 (top left), 24 (top), 27 (both), 28, 29 (bottom);
Peter Newark's Pictures: 5 (top), 9, 15 (bottom), 16
(bottom), 22; Topham: 15 (top); Plymouth Library
Services: 26; The Royal British Legion: 29 (top).
Thank you to Mrs J Keely, Robert Downey,
David Attlee and Audrey Knowles for providing
the personal photographs and artefacts in this
book.

Beat 'FIREBOMB FRITZ'

BRITAIN SHALL NOT BURN

BRITAIN'S FIRE GUARD IS BRITAIN'S DEFENCE

We can understand more about Britain during World War II by looking at the evidence left over from that period. There are bomb shelters, warships, fortresses, weapons, papers, pictures, and even gaps where bombed buildings once stood.

Many people who lived through the war are still alive. There may be people in your family who can talk to you about their part in the war. Their memories could provide very special evidence as you follow on the trail of World War II in Britain.

▲ This wartime poster is encouraging people to help the fire-fighting services.

This field gun now stands on a roundabout outside an army barracks. It was used in battle during World War II.

WARTIME GOVERNMENT

During the war, the Prime Minister ran the country with the help of a few important ministers. They were known as the 'Cabinet'.

The Cabinet normally met in the Prime Minister's house at 10 Downing Street in London. But they also had a meeting place called the Cabinet War Rooms.

One look at the Cabinet War Rooms should tell you what they were for. They are built three metres below street level, between Parliament and Downing Street. A one-metre thick slab of concrete covers the roof. This was an enormous bomb shelter, designed as a safe meeting place for the country's most important ministers. If they had been killed by a bomb, Britain might have fallen into chaos.

▲ Prime Minister Winston Churchill often made inspiring radio broadcasts during the war. His words helped to keep people's spirits up.

This picture shows where the Cabinet met. Over the door are two light bulbs, one red, the other green. The red one came on when an air-raid was taking place above.

▲ The Map Room in the Cabinet War Rooms. The big maps on the wall showed where the fighting was taking place all round the world.

By thinking about the evidence that we find on the trail of World War II we can learn a great deal. There are bedrooms and bathrooms at the Cabinet War Rooms. This tells us that the ministers and their staff often had to stay on at work day and night, without going home at all.

Although there are pipes to bring in fresh air, the underground rooms are cramped and stuffy. Imagine what they were like during the war, when 60 ministers, secretaries, civil servants and leaders of the army, navy and air force lived and worked there.

WINSTON CHURCHILL
When World War II began, Britain's Prime Minister was Neville Chamberlain. Winston Churchill took over in 1940 and led the country until 1945. He was a tough, confident leader whose famous speeches gave people hope in difficult times.

Winston Churchill (second from the left in the front row) with his Cabinet of leading ministers.

THE WAR IN THE AIR

In the summer of 1940, the Germans planned to invade Britain. Before they could do this, they needed to destroy the Royal Air Force (RAF) that protected the country from the air.

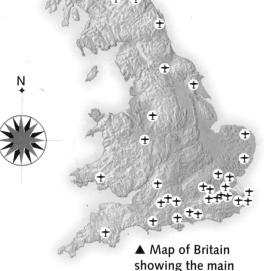

In July a huge air battle began over southern Britain - it was called the Battle of Britain. By September the Germans had lost hundreds of planes and the RAF still controlled the skies. Germany decided to postpone the invasion.

N

▲ Map of Britain showing the main wartime airfields.

SPITFIRES

The Spitfire was Britain's most modern fighter aircraft. It was fast and could turn very quickly. The bubble cockpit gave a good all-round view. When German bombers were on their way to Britain, Spitfire pilots took off and tried to attack from above. The people of Kent got to know the purring sound of the plane's Rolls Royce engine very well. It gave them hope, because they knew Spitfires usually got the better of the enemy.

A Supermarine Spitfire, Britain's fastest fighter, taking off from an airfield in Kent.

The Germans used dive-bombers in the Battle of Britain. The bomber's real name was Junkers Ju87, but everyone called it a 'Stuka'. You can see one at the Imperial War Museum in London. When a Stuka reached its target, it dived down in a straight line and dropped its bombs.

Stuka attacks were terrifying for the people on the ground because the planes had sirens which screamed as they dived. Actually, the pilots were in more danger than those on the ground. Stukas were slow and easy to shoot down. So many were lost that the Germans soon took them out of the battle.

▲ The 'Stuka' dive-bomber. The black crosses were the markings of the German airforce.

DEFENDING THE COAST

If the Germans had invaded Britain, some German soldiers would have crossed the Channel in boats. Others would have landed by parachute.

When the British found out about Germany's plans to invade, they built all kinds of defences. The strangest of these were around the port of Dover. The area was known as Hellfire Corner because it was bombed so often. If you ever sail into Dover, look carefully at the White Cliffs and you will see dark holes in the rock. These led to a network of tunnels which were part of Britain's most important World War II fortress. It is now open to the public.

▼ Hellfire Corner: the underground telephone exchange deep beneath the White Cliffs of Dover.

The tunnels were used by the Army to control all the guns along this part of the coast. Because they were deep underground, they were safe from air-raids. Nearby there were dormitories, a kitchen and even a hospital - all hollowed out of the chalk.

Have you ever seen one of these small concrete forts left over from World War II? They were known as 'pillboxes'. There are dozens of them still standing in the fields and woods of southern England. The openings were for guns. During the war, pillboxes had thick, steel doors at the back.

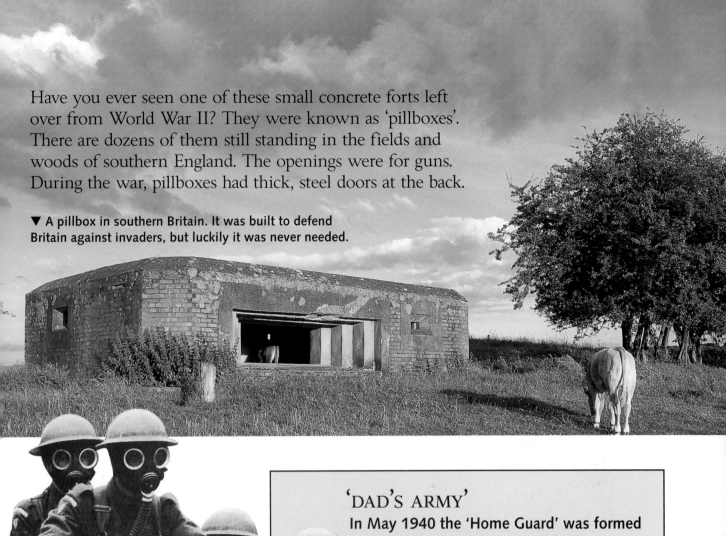

▼ A pillbox in southern Britain. It was built to defend Britain against invaders, but luckily it was never needed.

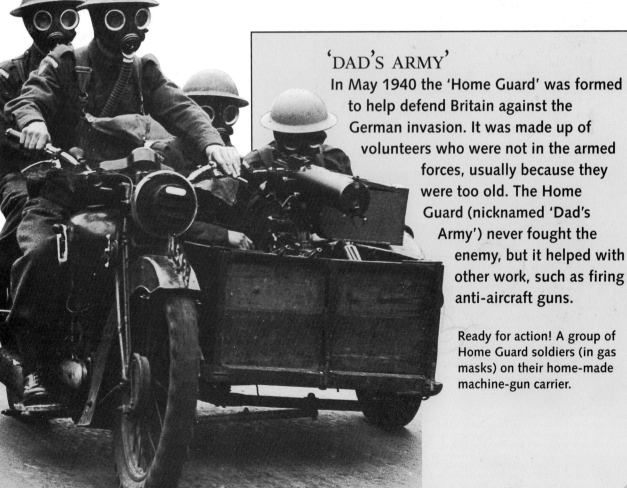

'DAD'S ARMY'

In May 1940 the 'Home Guard' was formed to help defend Britain against the German invasion. It was made up of volunteers who were not in the armed forces, usually because they were too old. The Home Guard (nicknamed 'Dad's Army') never fought the enemy, but it helped with other work, such as firing anti-aircraft guns.

Ready for action! A group of Home Guard soldiers (in gas masks) on their home-made machine-gun carrier.

THE BLITZ

During the war enemy bombing killed 40,000 people and destroyed 2 million homes.

A bombing raid (nicknamed a 'Blitz') brought the horrors of war right into the city centre. London was hardest hit. Bristol, Plymouth, Birmingham and Liverpool were also bombed several times.

This is all that remains of Coventry's splendid, medieval cathedral. It was once one of the most beautiful medieval buildings in Britain. During the night of 14-15 November 1940, Coventry was all but destroyed by high explosives and fire (or 'incendiary') bombs.

▼ Old and new: Coventry's modern cathedral rises out of the ruins of the one destroyed by enemy bombs.

Coventry was targeted because its factories produced weapons and military vehicles. But at night high-flying bombers could not aim accurately, so the cathedral and hundreds of houses were destroyed. Over 1,000 people were killed or badly injured.

The bombs started a blaze that swallowed up the whole city centre. Can you imagine the terrible roaring and smashing as the great cathedral and other buildings came crashing down? If you look at Coventry today, you will realise that almost all of the city centre had to be re-built after the war.

Glasgow
Newcastle
Sunderland
Middlesborough
Manchester
Hull
Liverpool
Sheffield
Nottingham
Birmingham
Coventry
Norwich
Swansea
Cardiff
London
Ipswich
Bristol
Bath
Southampton
Canterbury
Exeter
Portsmouth
Plymouth

▲ Cities that were hit hardest during the Blitz.

▼ Rescue workers search the wreckage of a bombed Liverpool school, 1940.

POUNDING THE PORTS
After the Battle of Britain, the Germans tried to make Britain surrender by cutting off its supplies of food and goods from abroad. Most of these arrived by ship and the bombers tried to smash the docks where the ships unloaded. This was why almost four times as many bombs fell on Liverpool as on nearby Manchester.

TAKING SHELTER

The first warning of an air-raid was the wailing noise of an air-raid siren. It must have been frightening to hear that eerie noise as you lay in bed.

Air-raid wardens told people what they should do when the siren sounded. You had to jump up, grab your gas mask and hurry through the dark to the nearest shelter.

It's safe down here: Londoners shelter from enemy bombs in the Elephant and Castle underground station.

If you have travelled on the London Underground, you might have visited the station above. But it wouldn't have looked anything like this. It is the Elephant and Castle station in 1940. The trains were stopped at night and the station became a bomb shelter.

BLACKOUT

At night Britain had a 'blackout' to make it hard for enemy bombers to find their way. No light was allowed to show outside. All street lights were switched off and people hung black material over their windows. Because car headlights were dimmed and road signs were unlit or removed, there were hundreds more traffic accidents.

A poster warning people to look where they were going in the blackout. At night wandering around the unlit streets could be very dangerous.

Families do their best to celebrate Christmas in a bomb shelter.

UNTIL YOUR EYES GET USED TO THE DARKNESS, TAKE IT EASY

LOOK OUT IN THE BLACKOUT

At the start of the Blitz, thousands of Londoners sheltered at night in the underground stations. Imagine being crowded together, clutching your belongings and wondering what was going on in the streets above.

The air below ground was foul and the toilets overflowed. Later, underground station shelters were better organised. Some had beds, canteens and even baths. People held sing-songs to drown out the noise of the guns and the bombs. In December, Father Christmas came to give presents to the children.

15

CAMP BEDS AND COCKROACHES

In September 1939, 1.5 million women and children moved from the cities to country towns and villages where they would be safe from bombs. This was called evacuation.

▶ Goodbye mum! Children, each one labelled, going off by train to the safety of the countryside.

▼ A wartime poster advises parents to get their children away from the dangers of the London Blitz.

LEAVE THIS TO US SONNY — **YOU** OUGHT TO BE OUT OF LONDON

MINISTRY OF HEALTH EVACUATION SCHEME

Many people went home again after a few weeks, but they were evacuated again when the Blitz began in 1940. A third evacuation took place in 1944, when London was attacked by missiles.

Although no children got lost during the evacuations, 38,000 never saw their parents again. Some parents were forced to move house or were killed. Others just abandoned their children.

During the war, Audrey Knowles was a schoolgirl in Redhill, near London. She stayed at home during the Blitz. Her school was bombed twice, and she spent most of the school day in an air-raid shelter. Later, when the missile attacks began, she was evacuated to South Wales. She was lucky that her mother and her younger sister went with her. Lots of children left their parents behind when they were evacuated.

'We were taken to a village hall', Audrey remembers, 'then sent out to our new homes. We were the last family to be picked and we went to a very big, old, damp house. There were cockroaches in our bedroom. The woman who lived there was very strict and spoke to us in Welsh - we didn't understand a word! We slept on camp beds and there weren't enough blankets. I got into trouble at school because I couldn't speak Welsh. I hated it and I cried a lot.'

▲ Audrey Knowles in her guide uniform, 1942. She was evacuated in 1944.

Audrey today. She still has vivid memories of World War II.

17

THE WAR AT SEA

During the war, the Germans tried to make the British surrender by starving them of food and other supplies.

The German plan could only succeed if the ships carrying food could be stopped from reaching British ports.

HMS *Belfast* is a World War II cruiser. Now safely moored on the Thames in central London, it is the only surviving warship of its kind. One of the jobs of the *Belfast* was to protect the ships carrying supplies to Britain. These ships were in danger of being attacked by German submarines. The work of the *Belfast's* crew was frightening, dangerous and uncomfortable.

The cruiser HMS Belfast anchored in the Thames, London. It is now a floating museum of naval life during World War II.

In 1939 HMS *Belfast* was blown up by a mine which put it out of action for over two years. After it was repaired, it escorted a convoy of ships to Russia.

It was not unusual for the ship to sail through hurricane conditions in these Arctic waters, and to battle with waves over 15m (50 feet) high.

There were 950 men in HMS *Belfast's* crew. They had everything they needed on board, although their living conditions were very cramped during the war. There was a dental officer and a ship's surgeon to look after their health. The ship had its own baker and butcher, there was a chapel and laundry. There was even a ship's cat to keep down the mice!

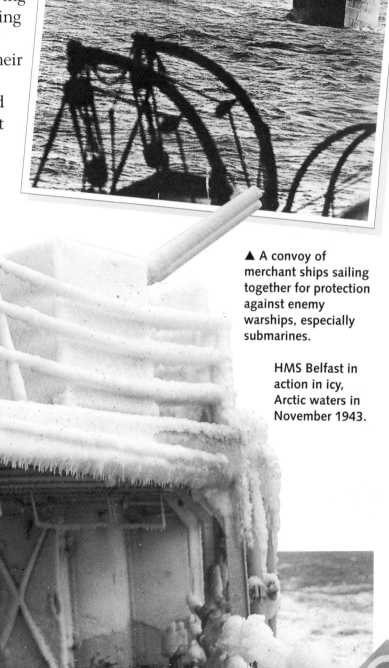

▲ A convoy of merchant ships sailing together for protection against enemy warships, especially submarines.

HMS Belfast in action in icy, Arctic waters in November 1943.

DIGGING FOR VICTORY

Despite the work of vessels like HMS *Belfast*, enemy warships and submarines sunk hundreds of ships bringing food and general supplies to Britain.

A fruit stall selling mostly home-grown produce. During the war banana ships were needed for carrying more important goods, such as weapons and grain.

The government had to make sure that everyone in Britain got their share of the foods that were in short supply. Rationing was introduced. This meant that each person was allowed to buy only a certain amount of some foods each week.

Other things, such as petrol and clothes were rationed, too. The government gave everyone a ration book so shopkeepers could check that people were only taking their fair share.

Luxuries such as sweets and exotic fruits like bananas and pineapples were not available at all. Some children did not taste them until after the war was over.

▲ Digging for victory: Clapham Common in South London was turned into an allotment in order to grow food during World War II.

▶ The green lawns of London's Clapham Common today.

Because of the loss of vital food supplies, the government encouraged people to use every possible piece of land for growing their own food. Crops and vegetables were grown in some very strange places.

The lower picture on this page shows Clapham Common in London today. The picture above it looks like an allotment, but is in fact Clapham Common during World War II. The Common was used for growing vegetables.

The government encouraged people to plant vegetables that grew well in Britain, such as carrots. To persuade them to grow more carrots, they started the rumour that eating carrots helped you see in the dark! Carrots never ran short, but some foods did. There often wasn't enough meat, eggs or sugar.

WOMEN AT WAR

During the war millions of men left their jobs to join the armed forces. Women took over their work and kept the country going. Other women joined special branches of the armed services.

For many women, this was their first experience of work outside the home. Some of them were surprised to find out how much they enjoyed their new responsibilities.

The Women's Land Army helped on farms. Their work was very important, but it was difficult to find enough women willing to join. Posters like this one tried to attract new recruits. Horses did the heavy work because all available fuel went to the army.

'We could do with thousands more like you..'

JOIN THE WOMEN'S LAND ARMY

A poster urging women to join the Land Army and help out on the farms.

Mrs Keely today (above left) and Mrs Keely with Italian prisoners of war (she is on the right) with whom she worked in the Timber Corps.

Mrs Keely was born near Liverpool and went to work with the Land Army in Herefordshire. 'Life seemed very old-fashioned,' she remembers. 'We lived in farmhouses. The toilets in one place were so awful that my friend refused to stay there.

We were in the Timber Corps, helping cut down trees that were used to make paper. We worked with Italian prisoners of war. We never really thought of them as the enemy. They were just nice people.'

HARD LABOUR

By 1945 some weapons ('munitions') factories were run almost entirely by women. Making things like tanks, shells and parachutes was quite well paid. But it was tough, dangerous work. Workers had to take care not to get their fingers or hair caught in the machinery, and some of the chemicals they handled made them ill.

Making ammunition in a munitions factory, 1943. The women had to tie their hair up in scarves to keep it out of the way.

SOUVENIRS OF WAR

All sorts of interesting objects are left over from the war. Many things, such as ration books, are still stored in lofts or at the bottom of drawers in people's homes. They are all evidence on the trail of World War II.

Some ex-service people still wear their campaign medals on Remembrance Sunday. These medals were awarded to a soldier who fought in North Africa. The oak leaf shows that he served with distinction.

GAS MASKS

Everyone had a gas mask – there were even special ones for babies! There are lots of gas masks still around today. They were worn during air-raids, in case poisonous gas bombs were dropped. Luckily, they never were.

People had to get used to wearing their gas masks while they went about their normal business.

Many people still have the medals that they were given as a reward for their hard work and bravery during the war. Ask your relations if you can see their medals. They may have a story to tell you about them.

Radios were vital during the war as they provided news about what was happening. Cheerful music and comedy shows kept people's spirits up. Wartime radios are still being used in some households. See if any of your relations have one.

Photographs are another clue on the trail of the World War II. Even if you have nothing in your family albums, you can often find pictures in antique shops or local history archives.

The War Medal 1939-1945

Most young service men and women were photographed in their uniforms. The pictures were kept at home by their loved ones.

You may find that your grandfather or your great-uncle still has his beret, like the one worn by the man on the left in this picture. Or he might have a steel helmet. These were given to people who needed protection against explosions. The broad brim was designed to protect people's faces. Otherwise, look out for uniforms and 'tin hats' at your local museum or antique shop.

WAR'S END

The War left Britain in a terrible state. The government had no money. Millions of soldiers, sailors and airmen had no jobs and thousands of buildings had been destroyed.

▼ Plymouth in the 1930s. Not one of these buildings was left after the bombing of February 1941.

The picture below shows the city of Plymouth in the 1930s. The picture opposite is of the same part of the city today. It's not difficult to see the difference. Before the war Plymouth had many historic buildings. Nowadays the city centre is almost entirely new.

A massive bombing raid in February 1941 almost completely flattened Plymouth. Can you imagine what it was like trying to clear up all the mess? Thousands of people were homeless. The water, electricity, gas and telephone supplies had been cut, and fires still smouldered among the ruins.

Plymouth was rebuilt after the war, following a careful plan. It became one of the most modern cities in the country, with ring roads for traffic and pedestrian precincts for shoppers.

Many years of rebuilding and repair followed the war. For people who had lost their homes or members of their families, life was never quite the same again.

Modern-day Plymouth. Almost the whole city had to be rebuilt after the war.

Factory-made prefabricated houses in Birmingham. These houses, supposed to be temporary, are still in use 50 years after they were put up.

PREFABS

As Britain was short of houses at the end of the war, thousands of factory-made concrete bungalows known as 'prefabs' (short for prefabricated) were built. The main pieces were carried to the building site and put together like a kit. They were meant to be used for only a short time, but they were very popular and some are still standing today.

One of Britain's thousands of war memorials honouring those who died in World Wars I and II.

REMEMBERING THE PAST

On 8 May 1945, Britain's role in the war in Europe came to an end. The British people went wild with relief. They took to the streets, singing and dancing, and parties went on long into the night.

The happiness was tinged with great sadness. During the war about half a million men, women and children from Britain and its empire had been killed.

Those who died during the World War II have not been forgotten. Have you ever worn a poppy?

DOUBLE BLOW

When World War I ended in 1918, the names of the dead were recorded on hundreds of war memorials. No one expected that the memorials would need altering. But after 1945 a new list of names was added – those who had died in World War II. The memorials are the saddest step on the trail of two terrible wars.

▲ The Remembrance Sunday service held each year before the Cenotaph war memorial in Whitehall, London.

▼ A 'Poppy Day' car sticker asking us not to forget those who died on our behalf in two World Wars.

REMEMBER THE DEAD — DON'T FORGET THE LIVING

R.B.L.Poppy Appeal Registered Charity

Have you been to a service on Remembrance Sunday, when a two minutes' silence is held? Perhaps you have watched a Remembrance Day parade. If you have done any of these things, you will have played your part in honouring the memory of those who lost their lives during World War II.

The custom of wearing poppies for Remembrance Day (11 November) began after World War I (1914-1918). It continued after World War II, when the dead from two World Wars were honoured. Now, over half a century later, we still wear poppies, and hold services and parades. As long as the custom continues, the trail of World War II will never grow cold.

GLOSSARY

air-raid
bomb attack from the air

allies
people fighting on your side in wartime

anti-aircraft guns
guns used for shooting at enemy aircraft from the ground

armed forces
army, navy and air force

blackout
hiding or turning out lights so that they cannot be seen from the air by enemy aircraft

Blitz
heavy bombing attack

Cabinet
chief ministers in the government

civil servant
someone employed by the government

cruiser
a medium-sized warship

evacuation
moving women and children from cities to the safety of the countryside in wartime

gas mask
mask that protects against poisonous gas

Home Guard
volunteer force set up to defend Britain against invasion

invade
enter an enemy country by force

mine
a bomb planted in the sea for blowing up ships

minister
person at head of government department

pillbox
small concrete fort with small holes for shooting out of

prefab
bungalow whose main bits, such as the walls, are made in a factory

rationing
government control of supplies, ensuring that everyone gets the same amount during times of shortage

ration book
book of coupons which were handed over when supplies were bought. This ensured that no one could buy more than their fair share of goods in short supply

volunteer
someone who chooses to do a job without being paid for it